The Poetry Of Hell

An Introduction.

It is often said that two things are unavoidable; Death and Taxes. Certainly the latter is a common thorn in adult life but as to the former it seems that for many people it is merely a hiccup in Life's eternal journey. A journey they wish, if being of good deed and character, to share at the eternity of Heaven's largesse, a reward for Faith and the obligations of Religion. Of course for those not so fortunate an altogether different experience was prepared for them; Hell. Its nightmare visions so terrifying conjured up by Dante and Milton. Here we have gathered together verse by such luminaries as William Blake, Charles Baudelaire, John Milton, Dante and, of course, many others to share their thoughts and vision.

Index Of Poems
Hades by Robert C O Benjamon
In Purgatory by John Bannister Tabb
Poe's Purgatory by John Bannister Tabb
Christ's Descent Into Purgatory, By Giorgione, At Venice by Richard Monckton Milnes Houghton
Love In Hades by Robert Crawford
Dance Of The Hanged Men by Arthur Rimbaud
The Day Of The Daughter Of Hades by George Meredith
The Caverns Of The Grave I've Seen by William Blake
The Devil's Drive: An Unfinished Rhapsody by Byron
A poem from Book Of Hours by Rainer Maria Rilke
A Convicts Tour to Hell by Francis McNamara
The Litanies Of Satan by Charles Baudelaire
Paradise Lost by John Milton (Extract)
Inferno – Canto III by Dante
The Marriage Of Heaven And Hell by William Blake

Hades by Robert C O Benjamon
Darkest clouds of blackest Hades,
Whirling onward into space;
Full of forms of ghostly horrors,
Madly join the phantom chase.

Earth below is lost in darkness,
Waves like mountains strike the sky,
Whilst the lurid lightning flashes,
And lost spirits shriek and cry.

Ne'er on earth was such dread darkness,
Ne'er such horrors, ghostly forms;
Ne'er such strokes of sulphurous lightning,
Ne'er such hellish terror storms.

And each vaporous home of thunder
Changed to aspect yet more dark;
And their crashing loud artillery
Followed close the 'lectric spark.

And each cloud with spirits damning,
Teemed till mountains filled their spheres,
And their hideous, ghostly laughter
Seemed devoid of hope and fears.

And their aspect seemed unnatural,
Devilish was their face and form;
Peals of shrieking, ghostly laughter
Quick increased, as did the storm.

Then that ghostly throng of spirits,
Each with death's marks on its brow,
Danced and kept tune to the thunders,
To the lightning's lurid glow.

Hark! the thunder crashes louder,
'Tis the ghostly spirits' band;
But above the deafening echoes
Are the curses of the damned.

Shuddering I, the scene beholding,
Felt my breast with horror swell;
For along the clouds in fire,
It was written - 'This is Hell!'

In Purgatory by John Bannister Tabb
'His sins were long ago forgiven;
So let him pass
at once
to heaven.'

Poe's Purgatory by John Bannister Tabb
All others rest; but I
Dream-haunted lie-

A distant roar,
As of tumultuous waters, evermore
About my brain.

E'en Sleep, tho' fain
To soothe me, flies affrighted, and alone
I bear the incumbent stone
Of Death
That stifles breath,
But not the hideous chorus crying 'Shame!'
Upon my name.

Had I not Song?
Yea; and it lingers yet
The souls to fret
Of an ignoble throng,
Aflame with hate
Of the exulting Fate
That hurls their idols from her temple fair,
And shrines me there.

Christ's Descent Into Purgatory, By Giorgione, At Venice by Richard Monckton Milnes Houghton
The saving work for man is finishèd,
The kingdoms of the Earth and Air o'erthrown;
So now hath Christ come down among the dead,
Spoiling the Spoiler, to redeem his own.
What blessèd glory plays about that head
For those who here in fiery bondage groan,
Conscious their suffering never could atone
For Sin, till He that once had sufferèd.
And, lo! in patient melancholy state
The synod of the Patriarchs rests apart
Condemned, tho' sons of God by faith, to wait
In this dark place and solitude of heart,
Joyless and tearless, till this Christ should come
To bear them to their Father and their Home.

Love In Hades by Robert Crawford
I saw Love pass with Charon down
The pale infernal tide,
To visit in the starless town
All who for him had died.
The gay God and the old Ghost came
Slow to that sleepy shore,

And a dead passion burned like flame
Before each true-love's door!
Into this place and that he stept:
The eyes still held their tears,
Though some had their strange sorrow kept
More than ten thousand years.
He saw the old and young who went
Devoid of life, yet who,
Though all their joys on earth were spent,
Were to their dream-loves true.
He saw all who had worshipped him
Before thought's light withdrew,
Until the ages seemed to swim
Round him there dying too!
And he could feel his faint heart beat
A ghostly tune with theirs,
As he, too, might cease to compete
With the decaying years.
Ay! though a God, he went aghast
From the mysterious shore,
And Charon smiled when he at last
Touched time with him once more.

Dance Of The Hanged Men by Arthur Rimbaud
On the black gallows, one-armed friend,
The paladins are dancing, dancing
The lean, the devil's paladins
The skeletons of Saladins.

Sir Beelzebub pulls by the scruff
His little black puppets who grin at the sky,
And with a backhander in the head like a kick,
Makes them dance, dance, to an old Carol-tune!

And the puppets, shaken about, entwine their thin arms:
Their breasts pierced with light, like black organ-pipes
Which once gentle ladies pressed to their own,
Jostle together protractedly in hideous love-making.

Hurray! the gay dancers, you whose bellies are gone!
You can cut capers on such a long stage!
Hop! never mind whether it's fighting or dancing!
- Beelzebub, maddened, saws on his fiddles!

Oh the hard heels, no one's pumps are wearing out!
And nearly all have taken of their shirts of skin;

The rest is not embarrassing and can be seen without shame.
On each skull the snow places a white hat:

The crow acts as a plume for these cracked brains,
A scrap of flesh clings to each lean chin:
You would say, to see them turning in their dark combats,
They were stiff knights clashing pasteboard armours.

Hurrah! the wind whistles at the skeletons' grand ball!
The black gallows moans like an organ of iron !
The wolves howl back from the violet forests:
And on the horizon the sky is hell-red...

Ho there, shake up those funereal braggarts,
Craftily telling with their great broken fingers
The beads of their loves on their pale vertebrae:
Hey the departed, this is no monastery here!

Oh! but see how from the middle of this Dance of Death
Springs into the red sky a great skeleton, mad,
Carried away by his own impetus, like a rearing horse:
And, feeling the rope tight again round his neck,

Clenches his knuckles on his thighbone with a crack
Uttering cries like mocking laughter,
And then like a mountebank into his booth,
Skips back into the dance to the music of the bones!

On the black gallows, one-armed friend,
The paladins are dancing, dancing
The lean, the devil's paladins
The skeletons of Saladins.

The Day Of The Daughter Of Hades by George Meredith
I

He who has looked upon Earth
Deeper than flower and fruit,
Losing some hue of his mirth,
As the tree striking rock at the root,
Unto him shall the marvellous tale
Of Callistes more humanly come
With the touch on his breast than a hail
From the markets that hum.

II

Now the youth footed swift to the dawn.
'Twas the season when wintertide,
In the higher rock-hollows updrawn,
Leaves meadows to bud, and he spied,
By light throwing shallow shade,
Between the beam and the gloom,
Sicilian Enna, whose Maid
Such aspect wears in her bloom
Underneath since the Charioteer
Of Darkness whirled her away,
On a reaped afternoon of the year,
Nigh the poppy-droop of Day.
O and naked of her, all dust,
The majestic Mother and Nurse,
Ringing cries to the God, the Just,
Curled the land with the blight of her curse:
Recollected of this glad isle
Still quaking. But now more fair,
And momently fraying the while
The veil of the shadows there,
Soft Enna that prostrate grief
Sang through, and revealed round the vines,
Bronze-orange, the crisp young leaf,
The wheat-blades tripping in lines,
A hue unillumined by sun
Of the flowers flooding grass as from founts:
All the penetrable dun
Of the morn ere she mounts.

III

Nor had saffron and sapphire and red
Waved aloft to their sisters below,
When gaped by the rock-channel head
Of the lake, black, a cave at one blow,
Reverberant over the plain:
A sound oft fearfully swung
For the coming of wrathful rain:
And forth, like the dragon-tongue
Of a fire beaten flat by the gale,
But more as the smoke to behold,
A chariot burst. Then a wail
Quivered high of the love that would fold
Bliss immeasurable, bigger than heart,
Though a God's: and the wheels were stayed,
And the team of the chariot swart

Reared in marble, the six, dismayed,
Like hoofs that by night plashing sea
Curve and ramp from the vast swan-wave:
For, lo, the Great Mother, She!
And Callistes gazed, he gave
His eyeballs up to the sight:
The embrace of the Twain, of whom
To men are their day, their night,
Mellow fruits and the shearing tomb:
Our Lady of the Sheaves
And the Lily of Hades, the Sweet
Of Enna: he saw through leaves
The Mother and Daughter meet.
They stood by the chariot-wheel,
Embraced, very tall, most like
Fellow poplars, wind-taken, that reel
Down their shivering columns and strike
Head to head, crossing throats: and apart,
For the feast of the look, they drew,
Which Darkness no longer could thwart;
And they broke together anew,
Exulting to tears, flower and bud.
But the mate of the Rayless was grave:
She smiled like Sleep on its flood,
That washes of all we crave:
Like the trance of eyes awake
And the spirit enshrouded, she cast
The wan underworld on the lake.
They were so, and they passed.

IV

He tells it, who knew the law
Upon mortals: he stood alive
Declaring that this he saw:
He could see, and survive.

V

Now the youth was not ware of the beams
With the grasses intertwined,
For each thing seen, as in dreams,
Came stepping to rear through his mind,
Till it struck his remembered prayer
To be witness of this which had flown
Like a smoke melted thinner than air,
That the vacancy doth disown.

And viewing a maiden, he thought
It might now be morn, and afar
Within him the memory wrought
Of a something that slipped from the car
When those, the august, moved by:
Perchance a scarf, and perchance
This maiden. She did not fly,
Nor started at his advance:
She looked, as when infinite thirst
Pants pausing to bless the springs,
Refreshed, unsated. Then first
He trembled with awe of the things
He had seen; and he did transfer,
Divining and doubting in turn,
His reverence unto her;
Nor asked what he crouched to learn:
The whence of her, whither, and why
Her presence there, and her name,
Her parentage: under which sky
Her birth, and how hither she came,
So young, a virgin, alone,
Unfriended, having no fear,
As Oreads have; no moan,
Like the lost upon earth; no tear;
Not a sign of the torch in the blood,
Though her stature had reached the height
When mantles a tender rud
In maids that of youths have sight,
If maids of our seed they be:
For he said: A glad vision art thou!
And she answered him: Thou to me!
As men utter a vow.

VI

Then said she, quick as the cries
Of the rainy cranes: Light! light!
And Helios rose in her eyes,
That were full as the dew-balls bright,
Relucent to him as dews
Unshaded. Breathing, she sent
Her voice to the God of the Muse,
And along the vale it went,
Strange to hear: not thin, not shrill:
Sweet, but no young maid's throat:
The echo beyond the hill
Ran falling on half the note:

And under the shaken ground
Where the Hundred-headed groans
By the roots of great AEtna bound,
As of him were hollow tones
Of wondering roared: a tale
Repeated to sunless halls.
But now off the face of the vale
Shadows fled in a breath, and the walls
Of the lake's rock-head were gold,
And the breast of the lake, that swell
Of the crestless long wave rolled
To shore-bubble, pebble and shell.
A morning of radiant lids
O'er the dance of the earth opened wide:
The bees chose their flowers, the snub kids
Upon hindlegs went sportive, or plied,
Nosing, hard at the dugs to be filled:
There was milk, honey, music to make:
Up their branches the little birds billed:
Chirrup, drone, bleat and buzz ringed the lake.
O shining in sunlight, chief
After water and water's caress,
Was the young bronze-orange leaf,
That clung to the tree as a tress,
Shooting lucid tendrils to wed
With the vine-hook tree or pole,
Like Arachne launched out on her thread.
Then the maiden her dusky stole
In the span of the black-starred zone,
Gathered up for her footing fleet.
As one that had toil of her own
She followed the lines of wheat
Tripping straight through the fields, green blades,
To the groves of olive grey,
Downy-grey, golden-tinged: and to glades
Where the pear-blossom thickens the spray
In a night, like the snow-packed storm:
Pear, apple, almond, plum:
Not wintry now: pushing, warm!
And she touched them with finger and thumb,
As the vine-hook closes: she smiled,
Recounting again and again,
Corn, wine, fruit, oil! like a child,
With the meaning known to men.
For hours in the track of the plough
And the pruning-knife she stepped,
And of how the seed works, and of how

Yields the soil, she seemed adept.
Then she murmured that name of the dearth,
The Beneficent, Hers, who bade
Our husbandmen sow for the birth
Of the grain making earth full glad.
She murmured that Other's: the dirge
Of life-light: for whose dark lap
Our locks are clipped on the verge
Of the realm where runs no sap.
She said: We have looked on both!
And her eyes had a wavering beam
Of various lights, like the froth
Of the storm-swollen ravine stream
In flame of the bolt. What links
Were these which had made him her friend?
He eyed her, as one who drinks,
And would drink to the end.

VII

Now the meadows with crocus besprent,
And the asphodel woodsides she left,
And the lake-slopes, the ravishing scent
Of narcissus, dark-sweet, for the cleft
That tutors the torrent-brook,
Delaying its forceful spleen
With many a wind and crook
Through rock to the broad ravine.
By the hyacinth-bells in the brakes,
And the shade-loved white windflower, half hid,
And the sun-loving lizards and snakes
On the cleft's barren ledges, that slid
Out of sight, smooth as waterdrops, all,
At a snap of twig or bark
In the track of the foreign foot-fall,
She climbed to the pineforest dark,
Overbrowing an emerald chine
Of the grass-billows. Thence, as a wreath,
Running poplar and cypress to pine,
The lake-banks are seen, and beneath,
Vineyard, village, groves, rivers, towers, farms,
The citadel watching the bay,
The bay with the town in its arms,
The town shining white as the spray
Of the sapphire sea-wave on the rock,
Where the rock stars the girdle of sea,
White-ringed, as the midday flock,

Clipped by heat, rings the round of the tree.
That hour of the piercing shaft
Transfixes bough-shadows, confused
In veins of fire, and she laughed,
With her quiet mouth amused
To see the whole flock, adroop,
Asleep, hug the tree-stem as one,
Imperceptibly filling the loop
Of its shade at a slant of sun.
The pipes under pent of the crag,
Where the goatherds in piping recline,
Have whimsical stops, burst and flag
Uncorrected as outstretched swine:
For the fingers are slack and unsure,
And the wind issues querulous:- thorns
And snakes!--but she listened demure,
Comparing day's music with morn's.
Of the gentle spirit that slips
From the bark of the tree she discoursed,
And of her of the wells, whose lips
Are coolness enchanting, rock-sourced.
And much of the sacred loon,
The frolic, the Goatfoot God,
For stories of indolent noon
In the pineforest's odorous nod,
She questioned, not knowing: he can
Be waspish, irascible, rude,
He is oftener friendly to man,
And ever to beasts and their brood.
For the which did she love him well,
She said, and his pipes of the reed,
His twitched lips puffing to tell
In music his tears and his need,
Against the sharp catch of his hurt.
Not as shepherds of Pan did she speak,
Nor spake as the schools, to divert,
But fondly, perceiving him weak
Before Gods, and to shepherds a fear,
A holiness, horn and heel.
All this she had learnt in her ear
From Callistes, and taught him to feel.
Yea, the solemn divinity flushed
Through the shaggy brown skin of the beast,
And the steeps where the cataract rushed,
And the wilds where the forest is priest,
Were his temple to clothe him in awe,
While she spake: 'twas a wonder: she read

The haunts of the beak and the claw
As plain as the land of bread,
But Cities and martial States,
Whither soon the youth veered his theme,
Were impervious barrier-gates
To her: and that ship, a trireme,
Nearing harbour, scarce wakened her glance,
Though he dwelt on the message it bore
Of sceptre and sword and lance
To the bee-swarms black on the shore,
Which were audible almost,
So black they were. It befel
That he called up the warrior host
Of the Song pouring hydromel
In thunder, the wide-winged Song.
And he named with his boyish pride
The heroes, the noble throng
Past Acheron now, foul tide!
With his joy of the godlike band
And the verse divine, he named
The chiefs pressing hot on the strand,
Seen of Gods, of Gods aided, and maimed.
The fleetfoot and ireful; the King;
Him, the prompter in stratagem,
Many-shifted and masterful: Sing,
O Muse! But she cried: Not of them
She breathed as if breath had failed,
And her eyes, while she bade him desist,
Held the lost-to-light ghosts grey-mailed,
As you see the grey river-mist
Hold shapes on the yonder bank.
A moment her body waned,
The light of her sprang and sank:
Then she looked at the sun, she regained
Clear feature, and she breathed deep.
She wore the wan smile he had seen,
As the flow of the river of Sleep,
On the mouth of the Shadow-Queen.
In sunlight she craved to bask,
Saying: Life! And who was she? who?
Of what issue? He dared not ask,
For that partly he knew.

VIII

A noise of the hollow ground
Turned the eye to the ear in debate:

Not the soft overflowing of sound
Of the pines, ranked, lofty, straight,
Barely swayed to some whispers remote,
Some swarming whispers above:
Not the pines with the faint airs afloat,
Hush-hushing the nested dove:
It was not the pines, or the rout
Oft heard from mid-forest in chase,
But the long muffled roar of a shout
Subterranean. Sharp grew her face.
She rose, yet not moved by affright;
'Twas rather good haste to use
Her holiday of delight
In the beams of the God of the Muse.
And the steeps of the forest she crossed,
On its dry red sheddings and cones
Up the paths by roots green-mossed,
Spotted amber, and old mossed stones.
Then out where the brook-torrent starts
To her leap, and from bend to curve
A hurrying elbow darts
For the instant-glancing swerve,
Decisive, with violent will
In the action formed, like hers,
The maiden's, ascending; and still
Ascending, the bud of the furze,
The broom, and all blue-berried shoots
Of stubborn and prickly kind,
The juniper flat on its roots,
The dwarf rhododaphne, behind
She left, and the mountain sheep
Far behind, goat, herbage and flower.
The island was hers, and the deep,
All heaven, a golden hour.
Then with wonderful voice, that rang
Through air as the swan's nigh death,
Of the glory of Light she sang,
She sang of the rapture of Breath.
Nor ever, says he who heard,
Heard Earth in her boundaries broad,
From bosom of singer or bird
A sweetness thus rich of the God
Whose harmonies always are sane.
She sang of furrow and seed,
The burial, birth of the grain,
The growth, and the showers that feed,
And the green blades waxing mature

For the husbandman's armful brown.
O, the song in its burden ran pure,
And burden to song was a crown.
Callistes, a singer, skilled
In the gift he could measure and praise,
By a rival's art was thrilled,
Though she sang but a Song of Days,
Where the husbandman's toil and strife
Little varies to strife and toil:
But the milky kernel of life,
With her numbered: corn, wine, fruit, oil
The song did give him to eat:
Gave the first rapt vision of Good,
And the fresh young sense of Sweet
The grace of the battle for food,
With the issue Earth cannot refuse
When men to their labour are sworn.
'Twas a song of the God of the Muse
To the forehead of Morn.

IX

Him loved she. Lo, now was he veiled:
Over sea stood a swelled cloud-rack:
The fishing-boat heavenward sailed,
Bent abeam, with a whitened track,
Surprised, fast hauling the net,
As it flew: sea dashed, earth shook.
She said: Is it night? O not yet!
With a travail of thoughts in her look.
The mountain heaved up to its peak:
Sea darkened: earth gathered her fowl;
Of bird or of branch rose the shriek.
Night? but never so fell a scowl
Wore night, nor the sky since then
When ocean ran swallowing shore,
And the Gods looked down for men.
Broke tempest with that stern roar
Never yet, save when black on the whirl
Rode wrath of a sovereign Power.
Then the youth and the shuddering girl,
Dim as shades in the angry shower,
Joined hands and descended a maze
Of the paths that were racing alive
Round boulder and bush, cleaving ways,
Incessant, with sound of a hive.
The height was a fountain-urn

Pouring streams, and the whole solid height
Leaped, chasing at every turn
The pair in one spirit of flight
To the folding pineforest. Yet here,
Like the pause to things hunted, in doubt,
The stillness bred spectral fear
Of the awfulness ranging without,
And imminent. Downward they fled,
From under the haunted roof,
To the valley aquake with the tread
Of an iron-resounding hoof,
As of legions of thunderful horse
Broken loose and in line tramping hard.
For the rage of a hungry force
Roamed blind of its mark over sward:
They saw it rush dense in the cloak
Of its travelling swathe of steam;
All the vale through a thin thread-smoke
Was thrown back to distance extreme:
And dull the full breast of it blinked,
Like a buckler of steel breathed o'er,
Diminished, in strangeness distinct,
Glowing cold, unearthly, hoar:
An Enna of fields beyond sun,
Out of light, in a lurid web;
And the traversing fury spun
Up and down with a wave's flow and ebb;
As the wave breaks to grasp and to spurn,
Retire, and in ravenous greed,
Inveterate, swell its return.
Up and down, as if wringing from speed
Sights that made the unsighted appear,
Delude and dissolve, on it scoured.
Lo, a sea upon land held career
Through the plain of the vale half-devoured.
Callistes of home and escape
Muttered swiftly, unwitting of speech.
She gazed at the Void of shape,
She put her white hand to his reach,
Saying: Now have we looked on the Three.
And divided from day, from night,
From air that is breath, stood she,
Like the vale, out of light.

X

Then again in disorderly words

He muttered of home, and was mute,
With the heart of the cowering birds
Ere they burst off the fowler's foot.
He gave her some redness that streamed
Through her limbs in a flitting glow.
The sigh of our life she seemed,
The bliss of it clothing in woe.
Frailer than flower when the round
Of the sickle encircles it: strong
To tell of the things profound,
Our inmost uttering song,
Unspoken. So stood she awhile
In the gloom of the terror afield,
And the silence about her smile
Said more than of tongue is revealed.
I have breathed: I have gazed: I have been:
It said: and not joylessly shone
The remembrance of light through the screen
Of a face that seemed shadow and stone.
She led the youth trembling, appalled,
To the lake-banks he saw sink and rise
Like a panic-struck breast. Then she called,
And the hurricane blackness had eyes.
It launched like the Thunderer's bolt.
Pale she drooped, and the youth by her side
Would have clasped her and dared a revolt
Sacrilegious as ever defied
High Olympus, but vainly for strength
His compassionate heart shook a frame
Stricken rigid to ice all its length.
On amain the black traveller came.
Lo, a chariot, cleaving the storm,
Clove the fountaining lake with a plough,
And the lord of the steeds was in form
He, the God of implacable brow,
Darkness: he: he in person: he raged
Through the wave like a boar of the wilds
From the hunters and hounds disengaged,
And a name shouted hoarsely: his child's.
Horror melted in anguish to hear.
Lo, the wave hissed apart for the path
Of the terrible Charioteer,
With the foam and torn features of wrath,
Hurled aloft on each arm in a sheet;
And the steeds clove it, rushing at land
Like the teeth of the famished at meat.
Then he swept out his hand.

XI

This, no more, doth Callistes recall:
He saw, ere he dropped in swoon,
On the maiden the chariot fall,
As a thundercloud swings on the moon.
Forth, free of the deluge, one cry
From the vanishing gallop rose clear:
And: Skiegeneia! the sky
Rang; Skiegeneia! the sphere.
And she left him therewith, to rejoice,
Repine, yearn, and know not his aim,
The life of their day in her voice,
Left her life in her name.

XII

Now the valley in ruin of fields
And fair meadowland, showing at eve
Like the spear-pitted warrior's shields
After battle, bade men believe
That no other than wrathfullest God
Had been loose on her beautiful breast,
Where the flowery grass was clod,
Wheat and vine as a trailing nest.
The valley, discreet in grief,
Disclosed but the open truth,
And Enna had hope of the sheaf:
There was none for the desolate youth
Devoted to mourn and to crave.
Of the secret he had divined
Of his friend of a day would he rave:
How for light of our earth she pined:
For the olive, the vine and the wheat,
Burning through with inherited fire:
And when Mother went Mother to meet,
She was prompted by simple desire
In the day-destined car to have place
At the skirts of the Goddess, unseen,
And be drawn to the dear earth's face.
She was fire for the blue and the green
Of our earth, dark fire; athirst
As a seed of her bosom for dawn,
White air that had robed and nursed
Her mother. Now was she gone
With the Silent, the God without tear,

Like a bud peeping out of its sheath
To be sundered and stamped with the sere.
And Callistes to her beneath,
As she to our beams, extinct,
Strained arms: he was shade of her shade.
In division so were they linked.
But the song which had betrayed
Her flight to the cavernous ear
For its own keenly wakeful: that song
Of the sowing and reaping, and cheer
Of the husbandman's heart made strong
Through droughts and deluging rains
With his faith in the Great Mother's love:
O the joy of the breath she sustains,
And the lyre of the light above,
And the first rapt vision of Good,
And the fresh young sense of Sweet:
That song the youth ever pursued
In the track of her footing fleet.
For men to be profited much
By her day upon earth did he sing:
Of her voice, and her steps, and her touch
On the blossoms of tender Spring,
Immortal: and how in her soul
She is with them, and tearless abides,
Folding grain of a love for one goal
In patience, past flowing of tides.
And if unto him she was tears,
He wept not: he wasted within:
Seeming sane in the song, to his peers,
Only crazed where the cravings begin.
Our Lady of Gifts prized he less
Than her issue in darkness: the dim
Lost Skiegencia's caress
Of our earth made it richest for him.
And for that was a curse on him raised,
And he withered rathe, dry to his prime,
Though the bounteous Giver be praised
Through the island with rites of old time
Exceedingly fervent, and reaped
Veneration for teachings devout,
Pious hymns when the corn-sheaves are heaped
And the wine-presses ruddily spout,
And the olive and apple are juice
At a touch light as hers lost below.
Whatsoever to men is of use
Sprang his worship of them who bestow,

In a measure of songs unexcelled:
But that soul loving earth and the sun
From her home of the shadows he held
For his beacon where beam there is none:
And to join her, or have her brought back,
In his frenzy the singer would call,
Till he followed where never was track,
On the path trod of all.

The Caverns Of The Grave I've Seen by William Blake

The Caverns of the Grave I've seen,
And these I show'd to England's Queen.
But now the Caves of Hell I view,
Who shall I dare to show them to?
What mighty soul in Beauty's form
Shall dauntless view the infernal storm?
Egremont's Countess can control
The flames of Hell that round me roll;
If she refuse, I still go on
Till the Heavens and Earth are gone,
Still admir'd by noble minds,
Follow'd by Envy on the winds,
Re-engrav'd time after time,
Ever in their youthful prime,
My designs unchang'd remain.
Time may rage, but rage in vain.
For above Time's troubled fountains,
On the great Atlantic Mountains,
In my Golden House on high,
There they shine eternally.

The Devil's Drive: An Unfinished Rhapsody by Byron

The Devil return'd to hell by two,
And he stay'd at home till five;
When he dined on some homicides done in ragoût,
And a rebel or so in an Irish stew,
And sausages made of a self-slain Jew--
And bethought himself what next to do,
'And' quoth he, 'I'll take a drive.
I walk'd in the morning, I'll ride to-night;
In darkness my children take most delight,
And I'll see how my favourites thrive,

'And what shall I ride in?' quoth Lucifer then--
'If I follow'd my taste, indeed,

I should mount in a wagon of wounded men,
And smile to see them bleed.
But these will be furnish'd again and again,
And at present my purpose is speed;
To see my manor as much as I may,
And watch that no souls shall be poach'd away.
'I have a state-coach at Carlton House,
A chariot in Seymour Place;
But they're lent to two friends, who make me amends,
By driving my favourite pace:
And they handle their reins with such a grace,
I have something for both at the end of their race.
'So now for the earth to take my chance:'
Then up to the earth sprang he;
And making a jump from Moscow to France,
He stepp'd across the sea,
And rested his hoof on a turnpike road,
No very great way from a bishop's abode.

But first as he flew, I forgot to say
That he hover'd a moment upon his way,
To look upon Leipsic plain;
And so sweet to his eye was its sulphury glare,
And so soft to his ear was the cry of despair,
That he perch'd on a mountain of slain;
And he gazed with delight from its growing height,
Nor often on earth had he seen such a sight,
Nor his work done half as well:
For the field ran so red with the blood of the dead,
That it blush'd like the waves of hell!
Then loudly, and wildly, and long laugh'd he:
'Methinks they have here little need of me!'

But the softest note that soothed his ear
Was the sound of a widow sighing;
And the sweetest sight was the icy tear,
Which horror froze in the blue eye clear
Of a maid by her lover lying--
As round her fell her long fair hair
And she look'd to heaven with that frenzied air,
Which seem 'd to ask if a God were there!
And, stretch'd by the wall of a ruin'd hut,
With its hollow cheek, and eyes half shut,
A child of famine dying:
And the carnage begun, when resistance is done,
And the fall of the vainly flying!

But the Devil has reach'd our, cliffs so white,
And what did he there, I pray?
If his eyes were good, he but saw by night
What we see every day:
But he made a tour, and kept a journal

Of all the wondrous sights nocturnal,
And he sold it in shares to the Men of the Row,
Who bid pretty well--but they cheated him, though!

The Devil first saw, as he thought, the Mail,
Its coachman and his coat
So instead of a pistol he cock'd his tail,
And seized him by the throat:
'Aha!' quoth he, 'what have we here?
'Tis a new barouche, and an ancient peer!'
So he sat him on his box again, And bade him have no fear, But be true to his club, and stanch to his rein, His brothel, and his beer;
'Next to seeing a lord at the council board,
I would rather see him here.'

The Devil gat next to Westminster,
And he turn'd to 'the room' of the Commons;
But he heard, as he purposed to enter in there,
That 'the Lords' had received a summons;
And he thought, as a ' quondam aristocrat,'
He might peep at the peers, though to hear them were flat;
And he walk'd up the house so like one of our own,
That they say that he stood pretty near the throne.

He saw the Lord Liverpool seemingly wise,
The Lord Westmoreland certainly silly,
And Johnny of Norfolk - a man of some size--
And Chatham, so like his friend Billy;
And he saw the tears in Lord Eldon's eyes,
Because the Catholics would not rise,
In spite of his prayers and his prophecies;
And he heard - which set Satan himself a staring--
A certain Chief Justice say something like swearing.
And the Devil was shock'd - and quoth he, 'I must go,
For I find we have much better manners below:
If thus he harangues when he passes my border,
I shall hint to friend Moloch to call him to order.'

A poem from Book Of Hours by Rainer Maria Rilke
You darkness, from whence I spring
I love you more than all the fires that fence the world,
for the fire encircles everyone but excludes you from their sight,
But darkness draws everything to it:
shapes and flames and animals and myself,
how it enfolds them all – man and might
It might be that a great power moves in my vicinity
I believe in nights – nights are my certainty.

A Convicts Tour to Hell by Francis McNamara

You prisoners of New South Wales,
Who frequent watchhouses and gaols
A story to you I will tell
Tis of a convict's tour to hell.
Whose valour had for years been tried
On the highway before he died
At length he fell to death a prey
To him it proved a happy day
Downwards he bent his course I'm told
Like one destined for Satan's fold
And no refreshment would he take
"Till he approached the Stygian lake
A tent he then began to fix Contiguous to the River Styx
Thinking that no one could molest him
He leaped when Charon thus addressed him
Stranger I say from whence art thou,
And thy own name, pray tell me now,
Kind sir I come from Sydney gaol
My name I don't mean to conceal
And since you seem anxious to know it
On earth I was called Frank the Poet.
[Are you that person? Charon cried],
I'll carry you to the other side.
Five or sixpence I mostly charge
For the like passage in my barge
So stranger do not troubled be
For you shall have a passage free
Frank seeing no other succour nigh
With the invitation did comply
And having a fair wind and tide
They soon arrived at the other side
And leaving Charon at the ferry
Frank went in haste to Purgatory
And rapping loudly at the gate
Of Limbo, or the Middle State
Pope Pius the 7th soon appeared
With gown, beads, crucifix and beard
And gazing at the Poet the while
Accosts him in the following style
Stranger art thou a friend or foe
Your business here I fain would know
Quoth the Poet for Heaven I'm not fitted
And here I hope to be admitted
Pius rejoined, vain are your hopes
This place was made for Priests and Popes
Tis a world of our own invention
But friend I've not the least intention
To admit such a foolish elf
Who scarce knows how to bless himself
Quoth Frank were you mad or insane
When first you made this world of pain?
For I can see nought but fire

A share of which I can't desire
Here I see weeping wailing gnashing
And torments of the newest fashion
Therefore I call you silly elf
Who made a rod to whip yourself
And may you like all honest neighbours
Enjoy the fruit of all your labours
Frank then bid the Pope farewell
And hurried to that place called Hell
And having found the gloomy gate
Frank rapped aloud to know his fate
He louder knocked and louder still
When the Devil came, pray what's your will?
Alas cried the Poet I've come to dwell
With you and share your fate in Hell
Says Satan that can't be, I'm sure
For I detest and hate the poor
And none shall in my kingdom stand
Except the grandees of the land.
But Frank I think you are going astray
For convicts never come this way
But soar to Heaven in droves and legions
A place so called in the upper regions
So Frank I think with an empty purse
You shall go further and fare worse
Well cried the Poet since 'tis so
One thing of you I'd like to know
As I'm at present in no hurry
Have you one here called Captain Murray?
Yes Murray is within this place
Would you said Satan see his face?
May God forbid that I should view him
For on board the Phoenix Hulk I knew him
Who is that Sir in yonder blaze
Who on fire and brimstone seems to graze?
'Tis Captain Logan of Moreton Bay
And Williams who was killed the other day
He was overseer at Grosse Farm
And done poor convicts no little harm
Cook who discovered New South Wales
And he that first invented gaols
Are both tied to a fiery stake
Which stands in yonder boiling lake
Hark do you hear this dreadful yelling
It issues from Doctor Warden's dwelling
And all those fiery seats and chairs
Are fitted up for Dukes and Mayors
And nobles of Judicial orders
Barristers Lawyers and Recorders
Here I beheld legions of traitors
Hangmen gaolers and flagellators
Commandants, Constables and Spies

Informers and Overseers likewise
In flames of brimstone they were toiling
And lakes of sulphur round them boiling
Hell did resound with their fierce yelling
Alas how dismal was their dwelling
Then Major Morriset I espied
And Captain Cluney by his side
With a fiery belt they were lashed together
As tight as soles to upper leather
Their situation was most horrid
For they were tyrants down at the Norrid
Prostrate I beheld a petitioner
It was the Company's Commissioner
Satan said he my days are ended
For many years I've superintended
The An. Company's affairs
And I punctually paid all arrears
Sir should you doubt the hopping Colonel
At Carrington you'll find my journal
Legibly penned in black and white
To prove that my accounts were right
And since I've done your will on earth
I hope you'll put me in a berth
Then I saw old Serjeant Flood
In Vulcan's hottest forge he stood
He gazed at me his eyes with ire
Appeared like burning coals of fire
In fiery garments he was arrayed
And like an Arabian horse he brayed
He on a bloody cutlass leaned
And to a lamp-post he was chained
He loudly called out for assistance
Or begged me to end his existence
Cheer up said I be not afraid
Remember No. Three Stockade
In the course of time you may do well
If you behave yourself in Hell
Your heart on earth was fraught with malice
Which oft drove convicts to the gallows
But you'll now atone for all the blood
Of prisoners shed by Serjeant Flood.
Then I beheld that well known Trapman
The Police Runner called Izzy Chapman
Here he was standing on his head
In a river of melted boiling lead.
Alas he cried behold me stranger
I've captured many a bold bushranger
And for the same I'm suffering here
But lo, now yonder snakes draw near
On turning round I saw slow worms
And snakes of various kinds and forms
All entering at his mouth and nose

To devour his entrails as I suppose
Then turning round to go away
Bold Lucifer bade me to stay
Saying Frank by no means go man
Till you see your old friend Dr. Bowman
Yonder he tumbles groans and gnashes
He gave you many a thousand lashes
And for the same he does bewail
For Osker with an iron flail
Thrashes him well you may depend
And will till the world comes to an end
Just as I spoke a coach and four
Came in full post haste to the door
And about six feet of mortal sin
Without leave or licence trudged in
At his arrival three cheers were given
Which rent I'm sure the highest Heaven
And all the inhabitants of Hell
With one consent rang the great bell
Which never was heard to sound or ring
Since Judas sold our Heavenly King
Drums were beating flags were hoisting
There never before was such rejoicing
Dancing singing joy or mirth
In Heaven above or on the earth
Straightway to Lucifer I went
To know what these rejoicings meant
Of sense cried Lucifer I'm deprived
Since Governor Darling has arrived
With fire and brimstone I've ordained him
And Vulcan has already chained him
And I'm going to fix an abode
For Captain Rossi, he's on the road
Frank don't go till you see the novice
The magistrate from the Police Office
Oh said the Poet I'm satisfied
To hear that he is to be tied
And burned in this world of fire
I think 'tis high time to retire
And having travelled many days
O'er fiery hills and boiling seas
At length I found that happy place
Where all the woes of mortals cease
And rapping loudly at the wicket
Cried Peter, where's your certificate
Or if you have not one to show
Pray who in Heaven do you know?
Well I know Brave Donohue
Young Troy and Jenkins too
And many others whom floggers mangled
And lastly were by Jack Ketch strangled
Peter, says Jesus, let Frank In

For he is thoroughly purged from sin
And although in convict's habit dressed
Here he shall be a welcome guest.
Isiah go with him to Job
And put on him a scarlet robe
St Paul go to the flock straightway
And kill the fatted calf today
And go tell Abraham and Abel
In haste now to prepare the table
For we shall have a grand repast
Since Frank the Poet has come at last
Then came Moses and Elias
John the Baptist and Mathias
With many saints from foreign lands
And with the Poet they all join hands
Thro" Heaven's Concave (sic) their rejoicings rang
And hymns of praise to God they sang
And as they praised his glorious name
I woke and found 'twas but a dream.

The Litanies Of Satan by Charles Baudelaire
O you, the most knowing, and loveliest of Angels,
a god fate betrayed, deprived of praises,
O Satan, take pity on my long misery!
O, Prince of exile to whom wrong has been done,
who, vanquished, always recovers more strongly,
O Satan, take pity on my long misery!
You who know everything, king of the underworld,
the familiar healer of human distress,
O Satan, take pity on my long misery!
You who teach even lepers, accursed pariahs,
through love itself the taste for Paradise,
O Satan, take pity on my long misery!
O you who on Death, your ancient true lover,
engendered Hope – that lunatic charmer!
O Satan, take pity on my long misery!
You who grant the condemned that calm, proud look
that damns a whole people crowding the scaffold,
O Satan, take pity on my long misery!
You who know in what corners of envious countries
a jealous God hid those stones that are precious,
O Satan, take pity on my long misery!
You whose clear eye knows the deep caches
where, buried, the race of metals slumbers,
O Satan, take pity on my long misery!
You whose huge hands hide the precipice,
from the sleepwalker on the sky-scraper's cliff,
O Satan, take pity on my long misery!
You who make magically supple the bones
of the drunkard, out late, who's trampled by horses,
O Satan, take pity on my long misery!

You who taught us to mix saltpetre with sulphur
to console the frail human being who suffers,
O Satan, take pity on my long misery!
You who set your mark, o subtle accomplice,
on the forehead of Croesus, the vile and pitiless,
O Satan, take pity on my long misery!
You who set in the hearts and eyes of young girls
the cult of the wound, adoration of rags,
O Satan, take pity on my long misery!

The exile's staff, the light of invention,
confessor to those to be hanged, to conspirators,
O Satan, take pity on my long misery!
Father, adopting those whom God the Father
drove in dark anger from the earthly paradise,
O Satan, take pity on my long misery!

Paradise Lost by John Milton (Extract)
Is this the Region, this the Soil, the Clime,
Said then the lost Arch-Angel, this the seat
That we must change for Heav'n, this mournful gloom
For that celestial light? Be it so, since he
Who now is Sovran can dispose and bid
What shall be right: fardest from him is best
Whom reason hath equald, force hath made supream
Above his equals. Farewel happy Fields
Where Joy for ever dwells: Hail horrours, hail
Infernal world, and thou profoundest Hell
Receive thy new Possessor: One who brings
A mind not to be chang'd by Place or Time.
The mind is its own place, and in it self
Can make a Heav'n of Hell, a Hell of Heav'n.
What matter where, if I be still the same,
And what I should be, all but less then he
Whom Thunder hath made greater? Here at least
We shall be free; th' Almighty hath not built
Here for his envy, will not drive us hence:
Here we may reign secure, and in my choyce
To reign is worth ambition though in Hell:
Better to reign in Hell, then serve in Heav'n.
But wherefore let we then our faithful friends,
Th' associates and copartners of our loss
Lye thus astonisht on th' oblivious Pool,
And call them not to share with us their part
In this unhappy Mansion, or once more
With rallied Arms to try what may be yet
Regaind in Heav'n, or what more lost in Hell?
So Satan spake, and him Beelzebub
Thus answer'd. Leader of those Armies bright,
Which but th' Onmipotent none could have foyld,
If once they hear that voyce, thir liveliest pledge

Of hope in fears and dangers, heard so oft
In worst extreams, and on the perilous edge
Of battel when it rag'd, in all assaults
Thir surest signal, they will soon resume
New courage and revive, though now they lye
Groveling and prostrate on yon Lake of Fire,
As we erewhile, astounded and amaz'd,
No wonder, fall'n such a pernicious highth.
He scarce had ceas't when the superiour Fiend
Was moving toward the shoar; his ponderous shield
Ethereal temper, massy, large and round,
Behind him cast; the broad circumference
Hung on his shoulders like the Moon, whose Orb
Through Optic Glass the Tuscan Artist views
At Ev'ning from the top of Fesole,
Or in Valdarno, to descry new Lands,
Rivers or Mountains in her spotty Globe.
His Spear, to equal which the tallest Pine
Hewn on Norwegian hills, to be the Mast
Of some great Ammiral, were but a wand,
He walkt with to support uneasie steps
Over the burning Marle, not like those steps
On Heavens Azure, and the torrid Clime
Smote on him sore besides, vaulted with Fire;
Nathless he so endur'd, till on the Beach
Of that inflamed Sea, he stood and call'd
His Legions, Angel Forms, who lay intrans't
Thick as Autumnal Leaves that strow the Brooks
In Vallombrosa, where th' Etrurian shades
High overarch't imbowr; or scatterd sedge
Afloat, when with fierce Winds Orion arm'd
Hath vext the Red-Sea Coast, whose waves orethrew
Busiris and his Memphian Chivalry,
While with perfidious hatred they pursu'd
The Sojourners of Goshen, who beheld
From the safe shore thir floating Carkases
And broken Chariot Wheels, so thick bestrown
Abject and lost lay these, covering the Flood,
Under amazement of thir hideous change.
He call'd so loud, that all the hollow Deep
Of Hell resounded. Princes, Potentates,
Warriers, the Flowr of Heav'n, once yours, now lost,
If such astonishment as this can sieze
Eternal spirits; or have ye chos'n this place
After the toyl of Battel to repose
Your wearied vertue, for the ease you find
To slumber here, as in the Vales of Heav'n?
Or in this abject posture have ye sworn
To adore the Conquerour? who now beholds
Cherube and Seraph rowling in the Flood
With scatter'd Arms and Ensigns, till anon
His swift pursuers from Heav'n Gates discern

Th' advantage, and descending tread us down
Thus drooping, or with linked Thunderbolts
Transfix us to the bottom of this Gulfe.
Awake, arise, or be for ever fall'n.
They heard, and were abasht, and up they sprung
Upon the wing, as when men wont to watch
On duty, sleeping found by whom they dread,
Rouse and bestir themselves ere well awake.
Nor did they not perceave the evil plight
In which they were, or the fierce pains not feel;
Yet to thir Generals Voyce they soon obeyd
Innumerable. As when the potent Rod
Of Amrams Son in Egypts evill day
Wav'd round the Coast, up call'd a pitchy cloud
Of Locusts, warping on the Eastern Wind,
That ore the Realm of impious Pharaoh hung
Like Night, and darken'd all the Land of Nile:
So numberless were those bad Angels seen
Hovering on wing under the Cope of Hell
'Twixt upper, nether, and surrounding Fires;
Till, as a signal giv'n, th' uplifted Spear
Of thir great Sultan waving to direct
Thir course, in even ballance down they light
On the firm brimstone, and fill all the Plain;
A multitude, like which the populous North
Pour'd never from her frozen loyns, to pass
Rhene or the Danaw, when her barbarous Sons
Came like a Deluge on the South, and spread
Beneath Gibralter to the Lybian sands.
Forthwith from every Squadron and each Band
The Heads and Leaders thither hast where stood
Thir great Commander; Godlike shapes and forms
Excelling human, Princely Dignities,
And Powers that earst in Heaven sat on Thrones;
Though of thir Names in heav'nly Records now
Be no memorial blotted out and ras'd
By thir Rebellion, from the Books of Life.
Nor had they yet among the Sons of Eve
Got them new Names, till wandring ore the Earth,
Through Gods high sufferance for the tryal of man,
By falsities and lyes the greatest part
Of Mankind they corrupted to forsake
God thir Creator, and th' invisible
Glory of him that made them, to transform
Oft to the Image of a Brute, adorn'd
With gay Religions full of Pomp and Gold,
And Devils to adore for Deities:
Then were they known to men by various Names,
And various Idols through the Heathen World.
Say, Muse, thir Names then known, who first, who last,
Rous'd from the slumber, on that fiery Couch,
At thir great Emperors call, as next in worth

Came singly where he stood on the bare strand,
While the promiscuous croud stood yet aloof?
The chief were those who from the Pit of Hell
Roaming to seek thir prey on earth, durst fix
Thir Seats long after next the Seat of God,
Thir Altars by his Altar, Gods ador'd
Among the Nations round, and durst abide
Jehovah thundring out of Sion, thron'd
Between the Cherubim; yea, often plac'd
Within his Sanctuary it self thir Shrines,
Abominations; and with cursed things
His holy Rites, and solemn Feasts profan'd,
And with thir darkness durst affront his light.

Inferno – Canto III - by Dante
The gateway to the city of Doom. Through me
The entrance to the Everlasting Pain.
The Gateway of the Lost. The Eternal Three
Justice impelled to build me. Here ye see
Wisdom Supreme at work, and Primal Power,
And Love Supernal in their dawnless day.
Ere from their thought creation rose in flower
Eternal first were all things fixed as they.
Of Increate Power infinite formed am I
That deathless as themselves I do not die.
Justice divine has weighed: the doom is clear.
All hope renounce, ye lost, who enter here.
This scroll in gloom above the gate I read,
And found it fearful. "Master, hard," I said,
"This saying to me." And he, as one that long
Was customed, answered, "No distrust must wrong
Its Maker, nor thy cowarder mood resume
If here ye enter. This the place of doom
I told thee, where the lost in darkness dwell.
Here, by themselves divorced from light, they fell,
And are as ye shall see them." Here he lent
A hand to draw me through the gate, and bent
A glance upon my fear so confident
That I, too nearly to my former dread
Returned, through all my heart was comforted,
And downward to the secret things we went.
Downward to night, but not of moon and cloud,
Not night with all its stars, as night we know,
But burdened with an ocean-weight of woe
The darkness closed us.
Sighs, and wailings loud,
Outcries perpetual of recruited pain,
Sounds of strange tongues, and angers that remain
Vengeless for ever, the thick and clamorous crowd
Of discords pressed, that needs I wept to hear,
First hearing. There, with reach of hands anear,

And voices passion-hoarse, or shrilled with fright,
The tumult of the everlasting night,
As sand that dances in continual wind,
Turns on itself for ever.
And I, my head
Begirt with movements, and my ears bedinned
With outcries round me, to my leader said,
"Master, what hear I? Who so overborne
With woes are these?"
He answered, "These be they
That praiseless lived and blameless. Now the scorn
Of Height and Depth alike, abortions drear;
Cast with those abject angels whose delay
To join rebellion, or their Lord defend,
Waiting their proved advantage, flung them here. -
Chased forth from Heaven, lest else its beauties end
The pure perfection of their stainless claim,
Out-herded from the shining gate they came,
Where the deep hells refused them, lest the lost
Boast something baser than themselves."
And I,
"Master, what grievance hath their failure cost,
That through the lamentable dark they cry?"
He answered, "Briefly at a thing not worth
We glance, and pass forgetful. Hope in death
They have not. Memory of them on the earth
Where once they lived remains not. Nor the breath
Of Justice shall condemn, nor Mercy plead,
But all alike disdain them. That they know
Themselves so mean beneath aught else constrains
The envious outcries that too long ye heed.
Move past, but speak not."
Then I looked, and lo,
Were souls in ceaseless and unnumbered trains
That past me whirled unending, vainly led
Nowhither, in useless and unpausing haste.
A fluttering ensign all their guide, they chased
Themselves for ever. I had not thought the dead,
The whole world's dead, so many as these. I saw
The shadow of him elect to Peter's seat
Who made the great refusal, and the law,
The unswerving law that left them this retreat
To seal the abortion of their lives, became
Illumined to me, and themselves I knew,
To God and all his foes the futile crew
How hateful in their everlasting shame.
I saw these victims of continued death
- For lived they never - were naked all, and loud
Around them closed a never-ceasing cloud
Of hornets and great wasps, that buzzed and clung,
- Weak pain for weaklings meet, - and where they stung,
Blood from their faces streamed, with sobbing breath,

And all the ground beneath with tears and blood
Was drenched, and crawling in that loathsome mud
There were great worms that drank it.
Gladly thence
I gazed far forward. Dark and wide the flood
That flowed before us. On the nearer shore
Were people waiting. "Master, show me whence
These came, and who they be, and passing hence
Where go they? Wherefore wait they there content,
- The faint light shows it, - for their transit o'er
The unbridged abyss?"
He answered, "When we stand
Together, waiting on the joyless strand,
In all it shall be told thee." If he meant
Reproof I know not, but with shame I bent
My downward eyes, and no more spake until
The bank we reached, and on the stream beheld
A bark ply toward us.
Of exceeding eld,
And hoary showed the steersman, screaming shrill,
With horrid glee the while he neared us, "Woe
To ye, depraved! - Is here no Heaven, but ill
The place where I shall herd ye. Ice and fire
And darkness are the wages of their hire
Who serve unceasing here - But thou that there
Dost wait though live, depart ye. Yea, forbear!
A different passage and a lighter fare
Is destined thine."
But here my guide replied,
"Nay, Charon, cease; or to thy grief ye chide.
It There is willed, where that is willed shall be,
That ye shall pass him to the further side,
Nor question more."
The fleecy cheeks thereat,
Blown with fierce speech before, were drawn and flat,
And his flame-circled eyes subdued, to hear
That mandate given. But those of whom he spake
In bitter glee, with naked limbs ashake,
And chattering teeth received it. Seemed that then
They first were conscious where they came, and fear
Abject and frightful shook them; curses burst
In clamorous discords forth; the race of men,
Their parents, and their God, the place, the time,
Of their conceptions and their births, accursed
Alike they called, blaspheming Heaven. But yet
Slow steps toward the waiting bark they set,
With terrible wailing while they moved. And so
They came reluctant to the shore of woe
That waits for all who fear not God, and not
Them only.
Then the demon Charon rose
To herd them in, with eyes that furnace-hot

Glowed at the task, and lifted oar to smite
Who lingered.
As the leaves, when autumn shows,
One after one descending, leave the bough,
Or doves come downward to the call, so now
The evil seed of Adam to endless night,
As Charon signalled, from the shore's bleak height,
Cast themselves downward to the bark. The brown
And bitter flood received them, and while they passed
Were others gathering, patient as the last,
Not conscious of their nearing doom.
"My son,"
- Replied my guide the unspoken thought - "is none
Beneath God's wrath who dies in field or town,
Or earth's wide space, or whom the waters drown,
But here he cometh at last, and that so spurred
By Justice, that his fear, as those ye heard,
Impels him forward like desire. Is not
One spirit of all to reach the fatal spot
That God's love holdeth, and hence, if Charchide,
Ye well may take it. - Raise thy heart, for now,
Constrained of Heaven, he must thy course allow."
Yet how I passed I know not. For the ground
Trembled that heard him, and a fearful sound
Of issuing wind arose, and blood-red light
Broke from beneath our feet, and sense and sight
Left me. The memory with cold sweat once more
Reminds me of the sudden-crimsoned night,
As sank I senseless by the dreadful shore.

The Marriage Of Heaven And Hell by William Blake

The Argument

Rintrah roars & shakes his fires in the burden'd air;
Hungry clouds swag on the deep.

Once meek, and in a perilous path,
The just man kept his course along
The vale of death.
Roses are planted where thorns grow,
And on the barren heath
Sing the honey bees.

Then the perilous path was planted:
And a river and a spring
On every cliff and tomb:
And on the bleached bones
Red clay brought forth.

Till the villain left the paths of ease,

To walk in perilous paths, and drive
The just man into barren climes.

Now the sneaking serpent walks
In mild humility,
And the just man rages in the wilds
Where lions roam.

Rintrah roars & shakes his fires in the burden'd air;
Hungry clouds swag on the deep.

As a new heaven is begun, and it is now thirty-three years since its advent: the Eternal Hell revives. And lo! Swedenborg is the Angel sitting at the tomb: his writings are the linen clothes folded up. Now is the dominion of Edom, & the return of Adam into Paradise: see Isaiah XXXIV & XXXV Chap:

Without Contraries is no progression. Attraction and Repulsion, Reason and Energy, Love and Hate, are necessary to Human existence.

From these contraries spring what the religious call Good & Evil. Good is the passive that obeys Reason. Evil is the active springing from Energy.

Good is Heaven. Evil is Hell

All Bibles or sacred codes, have been the causes of the following Errors.
1. That Man has two real existing principles Viz: a Body & a Soul.
2. That Energy, call'd Evil, is alone from the Body, & that Reason, call'd Good, is alone from the Soul.
3. That God will torment Man in Eternity for following his Energies.

But the following Contraries to these are True.
1. Man has no Body distinct from his Soul; for that call'd Body is a portion of Soul discern'd by the five Senses, the chief inlets of Soul in this age.
2. Energy is the only life and is from the Body and Reason is the bound or outward circumference of Energy.
3. Energy is Eternal Delight.

Those who restrain desire, do so because theirs is weak enough to be restrained; and the restrainer of reason usurps its place & governs the unwilling.

And being restrain'd it by degrees becomes passive till it is only the shadow of desire.

The history of this written in Paradise Lost, & the Governor of Reason is call'd Messiah.

And the original Archangel or possessor of the command of the heavenly host, is call'd the Devil or Satan and his children are call'd Sin & Death.

But in the Book of Job Miltons Messiah is call'd Satan.

For this history has been adopted by both parties.

It indeed appear'd to Reason as if Desire was cast out, but the Devils account is that the Messiah fell, & formed a heaven of what he stole from the Abyss.

This is shewn in the Gospel, where he prays to the Father to send the comforter or Desire that Reason may have Ideas to build on, the Jehovah of the Bible being no other than he who dwells in flaming fire.

Know that after Christs death, he became Jehovah.

But in Milton' the Father is Destiny, the Son, a Raio of the five senses, & the Holy-ghost, Vacuum!

Note. The reason Milton wrote in fetters when he wrote of Angels & God, and at liberty when of Devils & Hell, is because he was a true Poet and of the Devils party without knowing it.

A Memorable Fancy

As I was walking among the fires of hell, delighted with the enjoyments of Genius; which to Angels look like torment and insanity, I collected some of their Proverbs; thinking that as the sayings used in a nation, mark its character, so the Proverbs of Hell, shew the nature in Infernal wisdom better than any description of buildings or garments,

When I came home: on the abyss of the five senses, where a flat sided steep frowns over the present world, I saw a mighty Devil folded in black clouds, hovering on the sides of the rock, with corroding fires he wrote the following sentence now percieved by the minds of men, & read by them on earth.

> How do you know but ev'ry Bird that cuts the airy way,
> Is an immense world of delight, clos'd by your senses five?

Proverbs Of Hell

In seed time learn, in harvest teach, in winter enjoy.
Drive your cart and your plow over the bones of the dead.
The road of excess leads to the palace of wisdom.
Prudence is a rich ugly old maid courted by Incapacity.
He who desires but acts not, breeds pestilence.
The cut worm forgives the plow.
Dip him in the river who loves water.

A fool sees not the same tree that a wise man sees.
He whose face gives no light, shall never become a star.
Eternity is in love with the productions of time.
The busy bee has no time for sorrow.
The hours of folly are measur'd by the clock, but of wisdom: no clock can measure.

All wholsom food is caught without a net or a trap.
Bring out number weight & measure in a year of dearth.
No bird soars too high, if he soars with his own wings.
A dead body, revenges not injuries.
The most sublime act is to set another before you.
If the fool would persist in his folly he would become wise.
Folly is the cloke of knavery.
Shame is Prides cloke.

Prisons are built with stones of Law, Brothels with bricks of Religion.
The pride of the peacock is the glory of God.
The lust of the goat is the bounty of God.
The wrath of the lion is the wisdom of God.
The nakedness of woman is the work of God.
Excess of sorrow laughs. Excess of joy weeps.
The roaring of lions, the howling of wolves, the raging of the stormy sea, and the destructive sword, are portions of eternity too great for the eye of man.
The fox condemns the trap, not himself.
Joys impregnate. Sorrows bring forth.
Let man wear the fell of the lion, woman the fleece of the sheep.
The bird a nest, the spider a web, man friendship.
The selfish smiling fool, & the sullen frowning fool, shall be both thought wise, that they may be a rod.
What is now proved was once, only imagin'd.
The rat, the mouse, the fox, the rabbit: watch the roots; the lion, the tyger, the horse, the elephant, watch the fruits.
The cistern contains; the fountain overflows.
One thought, fills immensity.
Always be ready to speak your mind, and a base man will avoid you.
Every thing possible to be believ'd is an image of truth.
The eagle never lost so much time, as when he submitted to learn of the crow.

The fox provides for himself, but God provides for the lion.
Think in the morning. Act in the noon. Eat in the evening. Sleep in the night.
He who has suffer'd you to impose on him knows you.
As the plow follows words, so God rewards prayers.
The tygers of wrath are wiser than the horses of instruction.
Expect poison from the standing water.
You never know what is enough unless you know what is more than enough.
Listen to the fools reproach! it is a kingly title!
The eyes of fire, the nostrils of air, the mouth of water, the beard of earth.
The weak in courage is strong in cunning.
The apple tree never asks the beech how he shall grow, nor the lion, the horse, how he shall take his prey.
The thankful reciever bears a plentiful harvest.
If others had not been foolish, we should be so.
The soul of sweet delight, can never be defil'd.
When thou seest an Eagle, thou seest a portion of Genius, lift up thy head!
As the catterpiller chooses the fairest leaves to lay her eggs on, so the priest lays his curse on the fairest joys.
To create a little flower is the labour of ages.
Damn, braces: Bless relaxes.

The best wine is the oldest, the best water the newest.
Prayers plow not! Praises reap not!
Joys laugh not! Sorrows weep not!

The head Sublime, the heart Pathos, the genitals Beauty, the hands & feet Proportion.
As the air to a bird of the sea to a fish, so is contempt to the contemptible.
The crow wish'd every thing was black, the owl, that every thing was white.
Exuberance is Beauty.
If the lion was advised by the fox, he would be cunning.
Improvement makes strait roads, but the crooked roads without Improvement, are roads of Genius.
Sooner murder an infant in its cradle than nurse unacted desires.
Where man is not nature is barren.
Truth can never be told so as to be understood, and not be believ'd.
Enough! or Too much!

The ancient Poets animated all sensible objects with Gods or Geniuses, calling them by the names and adorning them with the properties of woods, rivers, mountains, lakes, cities, nations, and whatever their enlarged & numerous senses could percieve.

And particularly they studied the genius of each city & country, placing it under its mental deity.

Till a system was formed, which some took advantage of &enslav'd the vulgar by attempting to realize or abstract the mental deities from their objects; thus began Priesthood.

> Choosing forms of worship from poetic tales.
> And a length they pronounc'd that the Gods had order'd such things.
> Thus men forgot that All deities reside in the human breast.

A Memorable Fancy

The Prophets Isaiah and Ezekiel dined with me, and I asked them how they dared so roundly to assert, that God spoke to them; and whether they did not think at the time, that they would be misunderstood, & so be the cause of imposition.

Isaiah answer'd, I saw no God, nor heard any, in a finite organical perception; but my senses discover'd the infinite in every thing, and as I was then perswaded, & remain confirm'd; that the voice of honest indignation is the voice of God, I cared not for consequences but wrote.

Then I asked: does a firm perswasion that a thing is so, make it so?

He replied, All poets that it does, & in ages of imagination this firm perswasion removed mountains; but many are not capable of a firm perswasion of any thing.

Then Ezekiel said, The philosophy of the east taught the first principles of human perception: some nations held one principle for the origin & some another; we of Israel taught that the Poetic Genius (as you now call it) was the first principle and all other others merely derivative, which was the cause of our despising the priests & Philosophers of other countries, and prophecying that all Gods would at last be proved to originate in ours & to be the tributaries of the Poetic Genius; it was this that our great poet King David desired so fervently & invokes so patheticly, saying by this he conquers enemies & governs kingdoms; and we so loved our God, that we cursed in his name all deities of surrounding nations, and asserted that they had rebelled; from these opinions the vulgar came to think that all nations would at last be subject to the jews.

This said he, like all firm perswasions, is come to pass, for all nations believe the jews code and worship the jews god, and what greater subjection can be?
I heard this with some wonder, & must confess my own conviction. After dinner I ask'd Isaiah to favour the world with his lost works, he said none of equal value was lost. Ezekiel said the same of his.

I also asked Isaiah what made him go naked and barefoot three years?he answer'd, the same that made our friend Diogenes the Grecian.

I then asked Ezekiel, why he eat dung, & lay so long on his right & left side? he answer'd, the desire of raising other men into a perception of the infinite; this the North American tribes practise, & is he honest who resists his genius or conscience only for the sake of present ease or gratification?

The ancient tradition that the world will be consumed in fire at the end of six thousand years is true, as I have heard from Hell.

For the cherub with his flaming sword is hereby commanded to leave his guard at tree of life, and when he does, the whole creation will be consumed, and appear infinite, and holy whereas it now appears finite & corrupt.

This will come to pass by an improvement of sensual enjoyment.

But first the notion that man has a body distinct from his soul, is to be expunged: this I shall do, by printing in the infernal method, by corrosives, which in Hell are salutary and medicinal, melting apparent surfaces away, and displaying the infinite which was hid.

If the doors of perception were cleansed every thing would appear to man as it is, infinite.

For man has closed himself up, till he sees all things thro' narrow chinks of his cavern.

I was in a Printing house in Hell & saw the method in which knowledge is transmitted from generation to generation.

In the first chamber was a Dragon-Man, clearing away the rubbish from a caves mouth; within, a number of Dragons were hollowing the cave.

In the second chamber was a Viper folding round the rock & the cave, and others adorning it with gold, silver and precious stones.

In the third chamber was an Eagle with wings and feathers of air; he caused the inside of the cave to be infinite; around were numbers of Eagle like men, who built palaces in the immense cliffs.

In the fourth chamber were Lions of flaming fire raging around & melting the metals into living fluids.

In the fifth chamber were Unnam'd forms, which cast the metals into the expanse.

There they were reciev'd by Men who occupied the sixth chamber, and took the forms of books & were arranged in libraries.

The Giants who formed this world into its sensual existence and now seem to live in it in chains, are in truth, the causes of its life & the sources of all activity; but the chains are, the cunning of weak and tame minds, which have power to resist energy, according to the proverb, the weak in courage is strong in cunning.

Thus one portion of being, is the Prolific, the other, the Devouring: to the devourer it seems as if the producer was in his chains, but it is not so; he only takes portions of existence and fancies that the whole.

But the Prolific would cease to be Prolific unless the Devourer as a sea recieved the excess of his delights.

Some will say, Is not God alone the Prolific? I answer, God only Acts & Is, in existing beings or Men.

These two classes of men are always upon earth, & they should be enemies; whoever tries to reconcile them seeks to destroy existence.

Religion is an endeavour to reconcile the two.

Note. Jesus Christ did not wish to unit but to seperate them, as in the Parable of sheep and goats! & he says I came not to send Peace but a Sword.

Messiah or Satan or Tempter was formerly thought to be one of the Antediluvians who are our Energies.

An Angel came to me and said O pitiable foolish young man! O horrible! O dreadful state! consider the hot burning dungeon thou art preparing for thyself to all eternity, to which thou art going in such career.

I said, perhaps you will be willing to shew me my eternal lot & we will contemplate together upon it and see whether your lot or mine is most desirable.

So he took me thro' a stable & thro' a church & down into the church vault at the end of which was a mill: thro' the mill we went, and came to a cave, down the winding cavern we groped our tedious way till a void boundless as a nether sky appear'd beneath us, & we held by the roots of trees and hung over this immensity, but I said, if you please we will commit ourselves to this void, and see whether providence is here also, if you will not, I will? but he answer'd, do not presume O young-man but as we here remain behold thy lot which will soon appear when the darkness passes away.

So I remain'd with him sitting in the twisted root of an oak; he was suspended in a fungus, which hung with the head downward into the deep.

By degrees we beheld the infinite Abyss, fiery as the smoke of a burning city; beneath us at an immense distance was the sun, black but shining; round it were fiery tracks on which revolv'd vast spiders, crawling after their prey; which flew or rather swum in the infinite deep, in the most terrific shapes of animals sprung from corruption, & the air was full of them, &seem'd composed of them; these are Devils, and arc called Powers of the air. I now asked my companion which was my eternal lot? he said, between the black & white spiders.

But now, from between the black & white spiders, a cloud and fire burst and rolled thro' the deep, blackning all beneath, so that the nether deep grew black as a sea & rolled with a terrible noise; beneath us was nothing now to be seen but a black tempest, till looking east between the clouds & the waves, we saw a cataract of blood mixed with fire, and not many stones throw from us appear'd and sunk again the scaly fold of a monstrous serpent; at last to the east, distant about three degrees appear'd a fiery crest above the waves; slowly it reared like a ridge of golden rocks till we discover'd two globes of crimson fire, from which the sea fled away in clouds of smoke, and now we saw, it was the head of Leviathan; his forehead was divided into streaks of green & purple like those on a tygers forehead: soon we saw his mouth & red gills hang just above the raging foam tinging the black deep with beams of blood, advancing toward us with all the fury of a spiritual existence.

My friend the Angel climb'd up from his station into the mill; I remain'd alone, & then this appearance was no more, but I found myself sitting on a pleasant bank beside a river by moonlight hearing a harper who sung to the harp, & his theme was, The man who never alters his opinion is like standing water, & breeds reptiles of the mind.

But I arose, and sought for the mill & there I found my Angel, who surprised asked me how I escaped?

I answer'd, All that we saw was owing to your metaphysics; for when you ran away, I found myself on a bank by moonlight hearing a harper. But now we have seen my eternal lot, shall I shew you yours? he laugh'd at my proposal; but I by force suddenly caught him in my arms, & flew westerly thro' the night, till we were elevated above the earths shadow; then I flung myself with him directly into the body of the sun; here I clothed myself in white, & taking in my hand Swedenborgs volumes, sunk from the glorious clime, and passed all the planets till we came to saturn; here I staid to rest, & then leap'd into the void, between saturn& the fixed stars.

Here, said I! is your lot, in this space, if space it may be call'd. Soon we saw the stable and the church, & I took him to the altar and open'd the Bible, and lo! it was a deep pit, into which I descended driving the Angel before me; soon we saw seven houses of brick; one we enter'd; in it were a number of monkeys, baboons, & all of that species, chain'd by the middle, grinning and snatching at one another, but witheld by the shortness of their chains; however I saw that they sometimes grew numerous, and then the weak were caught by the strong, and with a grinning aspect, first coupled with & then devour'd, by plucking off first one limb and then another till the body was left a helpless trunk; this after grinning & kissing it with seeming fondness they devour'd too; and here & there I saw one savourily picking the flesh off of his own tail; as the stench terribly annoy'd us both we went into the mill, & I in my hand brought the skeleton of a body, which in the mill was Aristotles Analytics.

So the Angel said: thy phantasy has imposed upon me &thououghtest to be ashamed.

I answer'd: we impose on one another, & it is but lost time to converse with you whose works are only Analytics.

Opposition is true Friendship.

I have always found that Angels have the vanity to speak of themselves as the only wise; this they do with a confident insolence sprouting from systematic reasoning:

Thus Swedenborg boasts that what he writes is new; tho' it is only the Contents or Index of already publish'd books.

A man carried a monkey about for a shew, & because he was a little wiser than the monkey, grew vain, and conciev'd himself as much wiser than seven men. It is so with Swedenborg; he shews the folly of churches & exposes hypocrites, till he imagines that all are religious, & himself the single one on earth that ever broke a net.

Now hear a plain fact: Swedenborg has not written one new truth:
Now hear another: he has written all the old falshoods.

And now hear the reason. He conversed with Angels who are all religious, & conversed not with Devils who all hate religion, for he was incapable thro' his conceited notions.

Thus Swedenborgs writings are a recapitulation of all superficial, opinions, and an analysis of the more sublime, but no further.

Have now another plain fact: Any man of mechanical talents may from the writings of Paracelsus or Jacob Behmen, produce ten thousand volumes of equal value with Swedenborgs, and from those of Dante or Shakespear, an infinite number.

But when he has done this, let him not say that he knows better than his master, for he only holds a candle in sunshine.

Once I saw a Devil in a flame of fire, who arose before an Angel that sat on a cloud, and the Devil utter'd these words.

The worship of God is, Honouring his gifts in other men each according to his genius, and loving the greatest men best; those who envy or calumniate great men hate God, for there is no other God.

The Angel hearing this became almost blue, but mastering himself he grew yellow, & at last white pink & smiling, and then replied,

Thou Idolater, is not God One? & is not he visible in Jesus Christ? and has not Jesus Christ given his sanction to the law often commandments, and are not all other men fools, sinners, & nothings?

The Devil answer'd: bray a fool in a morter with wheat, yet shall not his folly be beaten out of him; if Jesus Christ is the greatest man, you ought to love him in the greatest degree; now hear how he has given his sanction to the law of ten commandments: did he not mock at the sabbath, and so mock the sabbaths God? murder those who were murder'd because of him? turn away the law from the woman taken in adultery? steal the labor of others to support him? bear false witness when he omitted making a defence before Pilate? covet when he pray'd for his disciples, and when he bid them shake off the dust of their feet against such as refused to lodge them? I tell you, no virtue can exist without breaking these ten commandments; Jesus was all virtue, and acted from impulse, not from rules.

When he had so spoken: I beheld the Angel who stretched out his arms embracing the flame of fire, & he was consumed and arose as Elijah.

Note. This Angel, who is now become a Devil, is my particular friend; we often read the Bible together in its infernal or diabolical sense which the world shall have if they behave well.

I have also: The Bible of Hell: which the world shall have whether they will or no.

One Law for the Lion & Ox is Oppression.

A Song Of Liberty

1. The Eternal Female groan'd! it was heard over all the Earth:
2. Albions coast is sick silent; the American meadows faint!
3. Shadows of Prophecy shiver along by the lakes and the rivers and mutter across the ocean. France rend down thy dungeon;
4. Golden Spain burst the barriers of old Rome;
5. Cast thy keys O Rome into the deep down falling, even to eternity down falling,
6. And weep.
7. In her trembling hands she took the new born terror howling;

8. On those infinite mountains of light, now barr'd out by the atlantic sea, the new born fire stood before the starry king!
9. Flag'd with grey brow'dsnows and thunderous visages the jealous wings wav'd over the deep.
10. The speary hand burned aloft, unbuckled was the shield, forth went the hand of jealousy among the flaming hair, and (Plate 26) hurl'd the new born wonder thro' the starry night.
11. The fire, the fire, is falling!
12. Look up! look up! O citizen of London, enlarge thy countenance; O Jew, leave counting gold! return to thy oil and wine; O African! black African! (go, winged thought, widen his forehead.)
13. The fiery limbs, the flaming hair, shot like the sinking sun into the western sea.
14 Wak'd from his eternal sleep, the hoary element roaring fled away;
I5. Down rush'd beating his wings in vain the jealous king; his grey brow'dcouncellors, thunderous warriors, curl'd veterans, among helms, and shields, and chariots, horses, elephants: banners, castles, slings, and rocks,
I6. Falling, rushing, ruining! buried in the ruins, on Urthona's dens;
17. All night beneath the ruins, then their sullen flames faded emerge round the gloomy King.
18. With thunder and fire: leading his starry hosts thro' the waste wilderness, (Plate 27) he promulgates his ten commands, glancing: his beamy eyelids over the deep in dark dismay,
19. Where the son of fire in his eastern cloud, while the morning plumes her Golden breast,
20. Spurning the clouds written with curses, stamps the stony law to dust, loosing: the eternal horses from the dens of night, crying,

Empire is no more! and now the lion & wolf shall cease

Chorus
Let the Priests of the Raven of dawn, no longer in deadly black, with hoarse note curse the sons of joy. Nor his accepted brethren, whom tyrant, he calls free: lay the bound or build the roof. Nor pale religious letchery call that virginity, that wishes but acts not!

For every thing that lives is Holy.

www.ingramcontent.com/pod-product-compliance
Lightning Source LLC
Chambersburg PA
CBHW061310040426
42444CB00010B/2579